D is for Disneyland

D is for Disneyland

The Unofficial Kids' Guide to the Happiest Place on Earth

Kelly Pope Adamson

Editor: Bob McLain
Layout: Artisanal Text

ISBN 978-1-941500-46-0
Printed in the United States of America

Theme Park Press | www.ThemeParkPress.com
Address queries to bob@themeparkpress.com

For Cambria:

As Cinderella's Fairy Godmother said, "Even miracles take a little time."

Contents

Introduction

"To all who come to this happy place—Welcome!"

These are the words of a famous man with a big imagination. Walt Disney was born over a hundred years ago, in 1901, and grew up in the small town of Marceline, Missouri. As a little boy, Walt was always coming up with story ideas and sketches. When he grew up, Walt left his home and took a train to California, where he opened his own studio and created such memorable characters as Mickey Mouse, Donald Duck, and Snow White. After Walt had his two daughters, he dreamt of a place where children and adults could play and have fun together. This was how the idea of Disneyland was born.

On July 17, 1955, Walt Disney opened the gates to a wonderland of yesterday, today, and tomorrow. Opening day wasn't easy, with wet cement, little water, and people trying to climb the fence, but Disneyland has carried on. Sixty years after the park opened, Disneyland now includes eight lands to explore—Main Street, U.S.A., Adventureland, New Orleans Square, Critter Country, Frontierland, Fantasyland, Mickey's Toontown, and Tomorrowland—while still keeping Walt's original dream alive...a place where children and adults can have fun and be young-at-heart...together.

Disneyland A to Z

Adventureland

A is for Adventureland, where stories unfold
of jungles and temples and destinations of old.
Climb a tree, take a cruise, talk to some birds—
whether in a forbidden temple or out, adventure's the word!

Quick Facts

- Type: Land, Original
- Attractions: Enchanted Tiki Room, Indiana Jones Adventure, Jungle Cruise, Tarzan's Treehouse
- Restaurants: Aladdin's Oasis, Bengal Barbecue, Tiki Juice Bar, Tropical Imports
- Unique Extras: Zebras
- Opened: July 17, 1955
- Location: Next to Frontierland / Main Street, U.S.A.

Alice in Wonderland

Follow the smile to go with the cat—
you may find a white rabbit or a man with a hat.
When having tea or playing with the Queen of Hearts,
the place where you end is the same as where you start.

Quick Facts

- Type: Character, Dark Ride
- Height: Any
- Opened: June 14, 1958
- Location: Fantasyland

Astro Orbitor

The gateway to Tomorrowland, these rockets let you fly.
You control the up and down—go up to the sky!
Be warned, the spinning motion may make your parents sick,
but if you're a kid, this ride is a kick!

Quick Facts

- Type: Interactive, Spinning
- Height: Any
- Opened: May 22, 1998
- Location: Tomorrowland

Autopia

If you thought you were too young to drive a car,
check out Autopia—the coolest racing attraction by far!
As you drive over freeways, it's not about who wins the race;
it's about the thrill of the drive, and the smile on your face!

Quick Facts

- Type: FASTPASS, Interactive, Original
- Height: Must be 32" or taller to ride
- Opened: July 17, 1955 (Variations: Fantasyland Autopia, Junior Autopia, Midget Autopia, Tomorrowland Autopia)
- Location: Tomorrowland

Big Thunder Mountain Railroad

Hold on to your glasses and hats,
as you ride a wild train through a cave full of bats.
The snakes and the goat will give you a thrill,
just watch out as you speed over the next hill!

Quick Facts

- Type: FASTPASS, Thrill Ride (Small Drops)
- Height: Must be 40" or taller to ride
- Opened: September 2, 1979
- Location: Frontierland

Big Thunder Ranch

If you're looking for a Wild West petting zoo,
the horses and goats of this ranch may just be for you!

Quick Facts

- Type: Interactive
- Height: Any
- Opened: June 27, 1986
- Location: Frontierland

Buzz Lightyear Astro Blasters

A special mission from Space Ranger Buzz Lightyear—
help take down evil at all costs, but have no fear!
To fight Evil Emperor Zurg, Buzz will give you a laser gun—
hit the lit targets to make your score higher and have fun!

Quick Facts

- Type: Character, Dark Ride, Interactive, Spinning
- Height: Any
- Opened: May 5, 2005
- Location: Tomorrowland

Casey Jr. Circus Train

C

Lions and tigers and bears—oh my!
Which animal to be—you decide.
Ride the train in the caboose, or the monkey or lion cage—
the scenery will make stories jump off the page.

Quick Facts

- Type: Original
- Height: Any
- Opened: July 31, 1955
- Location: Fantasyland

Chip 'n' Dale Treehouse

These two rascally chipmunks know how to have fun.
Climb up through their treehouse and see the sun!
At the top you'll find a great view of the town.
You'll even have fun climbing back down!

Quick Facts

- Type: Character, Interactive
- Height: Any
- Opened: January 24, 1993
- Location: Mickey's Toontown

Critter Country

Enter the home of Br'er Rabbit—but beware—
Br'er Fox and Br'er Bear are up to mischief there!
Whether you want to Splash or visit your favorite Pooh bear,
there's a bunch of animals waiting to greet you with care.

Quick Facts

- Type: Land
- Attractions: Davy Crockett's Explorer Canoes, The Many Adventures of Winnie the Pooh, Splash Mountain
- Restaurants: Harbour Galley, Hungry Bear Restaurant
- Opened: November 23, 1988 (Originally opened as Bear Country in 1972)
- Location: Next to New Orleans Square

Davy Crockett's Explorer Canoes

If you're willing to do your fair share,
you can fly across the water by Pirate's Lair.
Grab a paddle, hop aboard, and prepare to row;
this ride isn't about getting a free tow!

Quick Facts

- Type: Interactive, Water
- Height: Any
- Opened: May 19, 1971 (Originally opened as Indian War Canoes on July 4, 1956)
- Location: Critter Country

The Disney Gallery

If looking at beautiful Disney art is your thing,
this showcase of paintings will make you sing.

Quick Facts

- Type: Scenic
- Height: Any
- Opened: July 11, 1987 (originally located above Pirates of the Carribean in New Orleans Square)
- Location: Main Street, U.S.A. (Opera House)

Disneyland Monorail

If you want a bird's eye view of the park,
hop aboard one of these vehicles known as "Mark".
Red, blue, or orange; these vehicles fly—
you can see everything from this "highway in the sky"!

Quick Facts

- Type: Transportation
- Height: Any
- Opened: June 14, 1959
- Location: Tomorrowland (goes to Downtown Disney)

Disneyland Railroad

All aboard for this "grand circle tour" of Disneyland
past the Grand Canyon diorama full of sand.
You'll chug all the way around the park.
There are tunnels, so be warned if you're afraid of the dark.

Quick Facts

- Type: Original, Transportation
- Height: Any
- Opened: July 17, 1955 (originally known as Santa Fe and Disneyland Railroad)
- Location: Stations in Main Street, U.S.A., Mickey's Toontown, New Orleans Square, Tomorrowland

The Disneyland Story Presenting Great Moments with Mr. Lincoln

A marvel of Walt Disney's imagination,
this theater showcases the 16th president of our nation.
To see an Animatronic figure walk and talk;
Walt thought this would give people a good kind of shock!

Quick Facts

- Type: Show (Animatronic/Indoor)
- Height: Any
- Opened: July 18, 1965 (replaced by Disneyland: The First 50 Magical Years from 2005–2009)
- Location: Main Street, U.S.A. (Opera House)

Donald's Boat

If you've ever wondered where Donald Duck stays,
come on inside the *Miss Daisy* to play.
At first glance this may seem like an ordinary boat,
but this sailing vessel is next to Goofy's house, in a moat.

Quick Facts

- Type: Character, Interactive
- Height: Any
- Opened: January 24, 1993
- Location: Mickey's Toontown

Dumbo the Flying Elephant

If you ever wanted to fly on an elephant with a feather in his nose,
Choose the Dumbo of your liking and be lifted off your toes.
Up and down over Fantasyland you'll go—
this little elephant knows how to put on a show.

Quick Facts

- Type: Character, Interactive, Original, Spinning
- Height: Any
- Opened: August 16, 1955
- Location: Fantasyland

Enchanted Tiki Room

All the birds sing words in this special room
but watch out—a thunderstorm looms!
Sing along with the flowers, totems, and birds.
Tropical paradise is just songs away—haven't you heard?

Quick Facts

- Type: Show (Animatronic/Indoor)
- Height: Any
- Opened: June 23, 1963
- Location: Adventureland

Fantasy Faire

Next to Sleeping Beauty Castle is this quaint town.
Here no one is allowed to frown.
With a Royal Hall to meet princesses and a Royal show,
grab your friends and tell them, "Let's go!"

Quick Facts

- Type: Character Meet and Greet (Royal Hall), Show (Live—Royal Theatre)
- Height: Any
- Opened: March 12, 2013
- Location: Fantasyland

Fantasyland

Come and visit a magical land at the center of the park.
Hop in a ride vehicle and go through the dark.
To avoid lines and go with princesses every which way,
this land is a good place to start your day!

Quick Facts

- Type: Land, Original
- Attractions: Alice in Wonderland, Casey Jr. Circus Train, Dumbo the Flying Elephant, Fantasy Faire, and many more (see Appendix B for full list)
- Restaurants: Edelweiss Snacks, Maurice's Treats, Troubador Tavern, Village Haus Restaurant
- Unique Extras: Bibbidi Bobbidi Boutique, Sword in the Stone
- Opened: July 17, 1955
- Location: At the end of Main Street, U.S.A.

Fantasyland Theatre (Mickey and the Magical Map)

Join Mickey and friends for a magical stage show.
With princesses, heroes, and Mickey Mouse, no one will say no.

Quick Facts

- Type: Character, Show (Live)
- Height: Any
- Opened: June 23, 1995 (formerly known as Videopolis; opened in 1985)
- Location: Fantasyland

Finding Nemo Submarine Voyage

Go underwater as never before,
these subs are a great way to explore.
Wave hello to Nemo, and Marlin—his dad.
Looking through the circle windows sure is rad.

Quick Facts

- Type: Character, Dark Ride, Water
- Height: Any
- Opened: June 11, 2007 (originally open June 1959–September 1998 as Submarine Voyage)
- Location: Tomorrowland

Frontierland

Mosey on over for a slice of the Wild, Wild West. Cowboys and train rides are what this land does best. With an updated mining town adventure to explore, this land gives you more fun than ever before!

Quick Facts

- Type: Land, Original
- Attractions: Big Thunder Mountain Railroad, Big Thunder Ranch, and many more (see Appendix B for full list)
- Restaurants: Stage Door Café and many more (see Appendix A for full list)
- Unique Extras: Petrified Tree
- Opened: July 17, 1955
- Location: Between Adventureland and Fantasyland

Frontierland Shootin' Exposition

Grab a rifle and take a stand.

You're in charge now, so give a hand.

These guns are for taking targets out.

When you knock one down, you're sure to shout.

Quick Facts

- Type: $$, Interactive
- Height: Any
- Opened: March 29, 1985, as the Frontierland Shootin' Arcade (originally opened July 12, 1957, as the Shooting Gallery)
- Location: Frontierland

Gadget's Go Coaster

G

Join Chip 'n' Dale's gal pal on this wild ride,
as you soar over Toontown with a friend by your side.
Short and sweet, this is a great first coaster to try.
You'll be so sad it's over, you're sure to give a sigh.

Quick Facts

- Type: Character, Thrill Ride (Small Drops)
- Height: Must be 35" or taller to ride
- Opened: January 24, 1993
- Location: Mickey's Toontown

The Golden Horseshoe Stage

Come in to this show for some rootin', tootin' good fun.
Walt Disney himself loved this attraction a ton!

Quick Facts

- Type: Original, Restaurant, Show (Live)
- Height: Any
- Opened: July 17, 1955
- Location: Frontierland

Goofy's Playhouse

Bounce around in this interactive garden for fun,
while your parents sit and enjoy the sun.
Goofy calls this play area his house;
nothing wrong living next to a duck and across from a mouse!

Quick Facts

- Type: Character, Interactive
- Height: Any
- Opened: January 24, 1993
- Location: Mickey's Toontown

Haunted Mansion

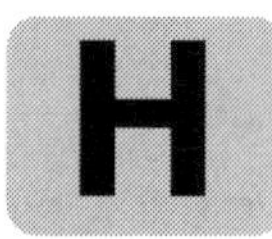

Enter into the stretching elevator if you dare.
Spooks and spirits reside here—beware!
Ride a Doom Buggy with those you hold dear;
just be careful when the hitchhiking ghosts come near.

Quick Facts

- Type: Dark Ride, Scary
- Height: Any
- Opened: August 9, 1969
- Location: New Orleans Square

Indiana Jones Adventure

Join the famous adventurer in a jeep.
Just watch out for things that crawl and creep.
If big snakes and spiders don't scare you,
get in line in this interactive queue!

Quick Facts

- Type: Dark Ride, FASTPASS, Scary, Thrill Ride (Small Drops)
- Height: Must be 46" or taller to ride
- Opened: March 3, 1995
- Location: Adventureland

Innoventions

The world of tomorrow awaits you here.
Learn about things of the future before they're near.
The interactive games will have you talking
and you'll be amazed to see a robot walking.

Quick Facts

- Type: Character Meet and Greet, Interactive (Indoor)
- Height: Any
- Opened: July 3, 1998
- Location: Tomorrowland

"it's a small world"

This boat ride celebrates every girl and boy.
Each country's singing is sure to bring you joy.
Enjoy a rainforest, a desert, and cities all in one ride.
These boats will carry you across the world's tides.

Quick Facts

- Type: Character, Dark Ride, Water
- Height: Any
- Opened: May 28, 1966 (originally opened at the New York World's Fair in 1964)
- Location: Fantasyland

Jungle Cruise

J

Grab your whole family and hop aboard a jungle boat.
When your guide isn't telling jokes, they'll keep you afloat.
Be amazed by the backside of water at Schweitzer Falls;
just to be sure to listen for the guide's danger calls.

Quick Facts

- Type: Original, Water
- Height: Any
- Opened: July 17, 1955
- Location: Adventureland

King Arthur Carrousel

Pick the horse of your choosing;
in this race there is no losing.
You'll have a blast on this merry-go-round.
Giggles and laughs will be your only sound!

Quick Facts

- Type: Original, Spinning
- Height: Any
- Opened: July 17, 1955
- Location: Fantasyland

Lines

L

Sometimes known as "queues", Disney makes these fun.
There's always something to look at while staying out of the sun.
In Indy, watch out for falling rocks.
And Thunder Mountain is sure to rock your socks!

Quick Facts

- Type: Scenic

Mad Tea Party

Get in one of these tea cups and go round and round.
Your parents will be so happy to get back to solid ground.
Take it slow or spin to go fast;
watch as Fantasyland twirls past.

Quick Facts

- Type: Interactive, Original, Spinning
- Height: Any
- Opened: July 17, 1955
- Location: Fantasyland

Magic Eye Theater (Captain EO)

This 3D show has awesome music and cool moves,
so sit back, relax, and get ready to groove.
This theater also shows previews of movies yet to be seen.
Kids of all ages can take a peek—from toddlers to teens.

Quick Facts

- Type: Show (Indoor/3D)
- Height: Any
- Opened: September 18, 1986 (closed in 1997 to make room for Honey, I Shrunk the Audience; re-opened February 23, 2010)
- Location: Tomorrowland

Main Street Cinema

When you're looking for a cool spot out of the sun, these classic Mickey Mouse cartoons provide shaded fun.

Quick Facts

- Type: Character, Original, Show
- Attractions: Any
- Opened: July 17, 1955
- Location: Main Street, U.S.A.

Main Street Vehicles

Ride in style, with or without a horse.

The Streetcars and Horseless Carriage follow the same course.

Take the Omnibus for a spectacular view.

The Fire Engine will carry you to the castle, too!

Quick Facts

- Type: Original, Transportation (Fire Engine, Horse-drawn Streetcars, Horseless Carriage, Omnibus)
- Height: Any
- Opened: Varied beginning July 17, 1955
- Location: Main Street, U.S.A.

Main Street, U.S.A.

Modeled after Walt Disney's hometown,
it's impossible to walk down this street with a frown.
With restaurants and shops galore,
this road will lead you to Fantasyland and more.

Quick Facts

- Type: Land, Original
- Attractions: Disneyland Railroad, Main Street Cinema, and many more (see Appendix B for full list)
- Restaurants: Carnation Café, Gibson Girl Ice Cream Parlor, and many more (see Appendix A for full list)
- Unique Extras: Fire Station, Partners, Windows
- Opened: July 17, 1955
- Location: Park entrance

The Many Adventures of Winnie the Pooh

Ride through the Hundred Acre Wood in a moving bee hive.
The Heffalumps and Woozles can be enjoyed by ages 100 to five.
Bounce along with Tigger and gather honey with Pooh.
The short lines for this attraction will make you happy, too.

Quick Facts

- Type: Character, Dark Ride
- Height: Any
- Opened: April 11, 2003
- Location: Critter Country

Mark Twain Riverboat

Sail the Rivers of America aboard this steamboat. Take in the sights on one of three decks as you float. Relax with your family during the 14-minute sail and listen to Mark Twain's interesting tale.

Quick Facts

- Type: Original, Water
- Height: Any
- Opened: July 17, 1955
- Location: Frontierland

Matterhorn Bobsleds

Conquer this mountain aboard a racing bobsled.
As you round each bend, look up ahead.
Watch out as you go for the roaring Yeti.
Buckle yourself in and make sure you're ready!

Quick Facts

- Type: Scary, Thrill Ride (Small Drops)
- Height: Must be 42" or taller to ride
- Opened: June 14, 1959
- Location: Fantasyland

Mickey's House and Meet Mickey

Toontown is the home of Mickey and his friends.
With the mouse who started it all, the fun never ends!
The mailbox outside lets you know this is Mickey's house.
Come inside to explore and meet the famous mouse.

Quick Facts

- Type: Character, Character Meet and Greet, Interactive
- Height: Any
- Opened: January 24, 1993
- Location: Mickey's Toontown

Mickey's Toontown

This cartoon land is home to Mickey and his pals.
All ages can enjoy this land, both guys and gals.
Silly sights like twisted lamp posts are all around.
You can even take your picture in a rubber pound!

Quick Facts

- Type: Land
- Attractions: Chip 'n' Dale Treehouse, Donald's Boat, Goofy's Playhouse, and many more (see Appendix B for full list)
- Restaurants: Clarabelle's Frozen Yogurt, Daisy's Diner, Pluto's Dog House
- Opened: January 24, 1993
- Location: Behind Fantasyland

Minnie's House

Minnie Mouse's house has an oven that bakes a cake and more.
Mickey's best gal pal has a house with so much to explore.
Come in and take a seat in the girl mouse's chair.
The details in this pink and purple house will make you stare.

Quick Facts

- Type: Character, Character Meet and Greet, Interactive
- Height: Any
- Opened: January 24, 1993
- Location: Mickey's Toontown

Mr. Toad's Wild Ride

This toad from *The Wind in the Willows* knows how to be wild.
A crazy car ride through Toad Hall is sure to get you riled.
Watch out for objects in the road as you zag and zig.
Mr. Toad gives you one crazy ride that you'll really dig.

Quick Facts

- Type: Dark Ride, Original, Scary, Spinning
- Height: Any
- Opened: July 17, 1955
- Location: Fantasyland

New Orleans Square

Follow the jazz music to this amazing bayou.
There are pirates and gumbo and musicians here, too.
If you feel like meeting some skeletons in the dark,
this land of fun and fright could be your favorite in the park.

Quick Facts

- Type: Land
- Attractions: Disneyland Railroad, Haunted Mansion, Pirates of the Caribbean
- Restaurants: Blue Bayou Restaurant, Café Orleans, and many more (see Appendix A for full list)
- Unique Extras: Club 33
- Opened: July 24, 1966
- Location: Between Adventureland and Critter Country

Omnibus

O

Taller than any other Disneyland ride vehicle, by far,
this double-decker bus is not your average car.
Down Main Street in style you'll go—
pretend you're royalty and wave to those below!

Quick Facts

- Type: Transportation
- Height: Any
- Opened: August 1956
- Location: Main Street, U.S.A.

Peter Pan's Flight

Follow the second star to the right
as you enjoy this magical flight.
In a pirate ship, fly over London and Mermaid Lagoon.
The wonder of this ride will make you come back soon.

Quick Facts

- Type: Character, Dark Ride, Original
- Height: Any
- Opened: July 17, 1955
- Location: Fantasyland

Pinocchio's Daring Journey

Ride through the streets with Pinocchio and Jiminy Cricket.
If you want to relive his story, this ride is the ticket.
Stick with Pinocchio as he overcomes Monstro the whale.
A real boy awaits you at the end of this tale.

Quick Facts

- Type: Character, Dark Ride, Scary
- Height: Any
- Opened: May 25, 1983
- Location: Fantasyland

Pirate's Lair on Tom Sawyer Island

Float on over to cross a rickety bridge or explore a cave.
The hidden treasures of this island will make you rave.
Find a lookout point and use the spyglass to watch out below.
The more you explore, the more you'll know!

Quick Facts

- Type: Interactive
- Height: Any
- Opened: May 25, 2007 (originally opened as Tom Sawyer Island on June 16, 1956)
- Location: Frontierland

Pirates of the Caribbean

Board a boat in this bayou with a shout of "Yo ho!"
The boat will take you downstream—just go with the flow.
Put your hands up on the drops and yell, "Whee!"
Soon you'll be saying, "It's the pirate's life for me!"

Quick Facts

- Type: Character, Dark Ride, Scary, Thrill Ride (Small Drops), Water
- Height: Any
- Opened: March 18, 1967
- Location: New Orleans Square

Pixie Hollow

Enter Tinkerbell's home amongst grass much taller than you. Tinkerbell waits to greet you with her fairy friends, too.

Quick Facts

- Type: Character Meet and Greet, Interactive
- Height: Any
- Opened: October 2008
- Location: Fantasyland

Questions and Answers

Use the Quick Facts to complete this quiz.

If you already know the answers—congrats! You're a whiz!

Q1: On what ride can you find tigers, elephants, and zebras? (Hint: Look under "Z".)

Q2: What ride did Big Thunder Mountain Railroad replace? (Hint: It's an attraction of "Yesterday".)

Q3: In which land is there a secret club?

Q4: Name one of the original attractions from 1955. (Hint: Check out Appendix C.)

A1: Jungle Cruise in Adventureland.

A2: Mine Train through Nature's Wonderland.

A3: New Orleans Square—Club 33.

A4: Autopia, Casey Jr. Circus Train, Disneyland Railroad, Dumbo the Flying Elephant, The Golden Horseshoe Stage, Jungle Cruise, King Arthur Carrousel, Mad Tea Party, Main Street Cinema, Main Street Vehicles, Mark Twain Riverboat, Mr. Toad's Wild Ride, Peter Pan's Flight, Sleeping Beauty Castle, Snow White's Scary Adventures, Storybook Land Canal Boats.

Roger Rabbit's Car Toon Spin

Get on board one of Roger's car friends and watch out for Dip.
All around this land of toons you're sure to slip.
Even the queue has lots of things to see.
Grab a FASTPASS for this attraction and a happy kid you'll be.

Quick Facts

- Type: Character, Dark Ride, FASTPASS, Spinning
- Height: Any
- Opened: January 26, 1994
- Location: Mickey's Toontown

Sailing Ship Columbia

S

Sail the Rivers of America with great flair.
Listen to the cannons shoot as you pass Pirate's Lair.
During Fantasmic! *Columbia* becomes Captain Hook's pirate ship,
but during the day, ride the rivers with a cannon at your hip.

Quick Facts

- Type: Water
- Height: Any
- Opened: June 14, 1958
- Location: Frontierland

Sleeping Beauty Castle

This landmark stands out above the rest.
Its turrets, banners, and moat make this castle the best.
Beware Maleficent as you learn Aurora's tale from a storybook,
the inside of Sleeping Beauty's Castle is definitely worth a look.

Quick Facts

- Type: Character, Original, Scenic
- Height: Any
- Opened: July 17, 1955 (Walkthrough opened April 29, 1957 (closed briefly from October 7, 2001, until November 28, 2008)
- Location: Fantasyland

Snow White's Scary Adventures

Travel along with Snow White as she meets her seven dwarfs. Gasp as you watch the Evil Queen use her potion to morph. Prince Charming awakens Snow White with a magical kiss, making this ride one not to miss.

Quick Facts

- Type: Character, Dark Ride, Original, Scary
- Height: Any
- Opened: July 17, 1955 (formerly known as Snow White's Adventures)
- Location: Fantasyland

Space Mountain

Watch out for falling asteroids as you blast through space.
This roller coaster thru the dark will put a smile on your face.
Zoom up, down, and over—you can't see the track!
You'll be so sad when the ride ends that you'll come right back.

Quick Facts

- Type: Dark Ride, FASTPASS, Scary, Thrill Ride (Large Drops)
- Height: Must be 40" or taller to ride
- Opened: May 4, 1977
- Location: Tomorrowland

Splash Mountain

On this log ride you'll sing along with Br'er Rabbit and friends.
Put your hands up and scream on the big drop toward the end.
If you sit in the front you may get soaked, but hey—
After a ride, you'll be singing "Zip-a-dee-doo-dah" all day.

Quick Facts

- Type: FASTPASS, Thrill Ride (Large Drops), Water
- Height: Must be 40" or taller to ride
- Opened: July 17, 1989
- Location: Critter Country

Starcade

Visit an out-of-this-world arcade for games from present and past. If you want to win here, you'll have to be fast.

Quick Facts

- Type: $$, Interactive
- Height: Any
- Opened: May 4, 1977
- Location: Tomorrowland

Star Tours—The Adventures Continue

Blast off to a galaxy far, far away.
Maybe have a different ride each time, even if you ride all day.
The motion of the room will make you feel like you're in space;
if you love *Star Wars*, this will be your new favorite place.

Quick Facts

- Type: Character, Dark Ride, FASTPASS, Thrill Ride (Small Drops)
- Height: Must be 40" or taller to ride
- Opened: January 9, 1987
- Location: Tomorrowland

Storybook Land Canal Boats

On this boat ride you will get to see classic Disney tales. Start out your ride by sailing through the mouth of a whale. Keep your hands in the boat as you sail past some real-life ducks. If you want to see Jasmine's home of Agrabah—you're in luck!

Quick Facts

- Type: Character, Original, Water
- Height: Any
- Opened: June 16, 1956 (Originally opened as Canal Boats of the World in 1955)
- Location: Fantasyland

Tarzan's Treehouse

T

Learn the story of Tarzan as you walk thru his home in the sky.
With so many things to look at, the time will fly by.
At the bottom, make some noise in his interactive camp.
Once you're done, you'll give this tree your approval stamp.

Quick Facts

- Type: Character, Interactive
- Height: Any
- Opened: June 23, 1999 (originally opened as Swiss Family Treehouse on November 18, 1962)
- Location: Adventureland

Tomorrowland

This land of the future is sure to make you grin.
As you walk in, stop and give the Astro Orbitor a spin.
Drive a car, take a dive, or fly through outer space;
in this land, the world of tomorrow awaits.

Quick Facts

- Type: Land, Original
- Attractions: Astro Orbitor, Autopia, Buzz Lightyear Astro Blasters, Finding Nemo Submarine Voyage, and many more (see Appendix B for full list)
- Restaurants: Redd Rockett's Pizza Port, The Spirit of Refreshment, Tomorrowland Terrace
- Opened: July 17, 1955
- Location: Between Main Street, U.S.A. and Fantasyland

Unique

Take a guess about where these unique spots might be;
when you think you have it, turn the book upside down to see!

Fire Station Location: Main Street, U.S.A.

Partners Location: Main Street, U.S.A. (Hub).

Petrified Tree Location: Frontierland.

Snow White Grotto Location: Fantasyland.

Unique: Fire Station

Above this fire house, a lamp burns bright.
The window into Walt's old apartment is a magical sight.

Quick Facts

- Type: Original, Scenic
- Height: Any
- Opened: July 17, 1955

Unique: Partners Statue

This statue honors Walt Disney—the man behind Disneyland.
And right next to him is Mickey Mouse, holding his hand.
Stop by and say hello to the man and the mouse;
after all, this amazing park is their house.

Quick Facts

- Type: Scenic
- Height: Any
- Opened: November 18, 1993

Unique: Petrified Tree

A gift from Walt Disney's wife, Lillian, to Disneyland,
In front of the Rivers of America, this fossil stands.

Quick Facts

- Type: Scenic
- Height: Any
- Opened: September 1957

Unique: Snow White Grotto

If you're looking for a dream to come true,
Snow White's wishing well is just for you.
Wave to the dwarfs as you throw your coin down
And imagine yourself in a majestic crown.

Quick Facts

- Type: Scenic
- Height: Any
- Opened: April 9, 1961

Village Haus Restaurant

Come into this quaint village restaurant for a quick bite to eat.
Inside or out, you're sure to find a seat.
It's the only place in the park to start with a "V".
But at pizzas and burgers, it's the best there can be.

Quick Facts

- Type: Restaurant
- Serves: Pizza, Salad, Sandwiches
- Opened: May 25, 1983
- Location: Fantasyland

Windows

W

When walking down Main Street, look toward the building tops.
A special surprise can be found above many of the land's shops.
These windows celebrate the people of Disney, present and past.
The clever decorations help these legend's legacies last.

Quick Facts

- Type: Scenic
- Height: Any
- Opened: Varied
- Location: Main Street, U.S.A.

Xtras

While Disneyland may not have any xylophones or x-rays to be found, there are plenty of extra special spots and experiences to go around!

Xtra: Bibbidi Bobbidi Boutique

They'll do your hair and makeup like a princess;
come out looking like Cinderella, even if you went in a mess!

Quick Facts

- Type: $$, Interactive
- Height: Any
- Opened: April 17, 2009
- Location: Fantasyland

Xtra: City Hall

If you're looking for a free button to celebrate your birthday, come on in to meet the friendly cast here and say, "Hey!"

Quick Facts

- Type: Original, Scenic (Guest Services)
- Height: Any
- Opened: July 17, 1955
- Location: Main Street, U.S.A.

Xtra: Club 33

A secret club makes its home in New Orleans Square.
With a long waiting list, you must be patient to eat there.

Quick Facts

- Type: Restaurant
- Serves: Upscale American
- Opened: June 15, 1967
- Location: New Orleans Square

Xtra: Sword in the Stone

If you think you're the strongest in the land,
step right up and try your hand.
Pulling out the sword is not as easy as it may seem.
But if you're the lucky one to do it, you're sure to beam.

Quick Facts

- Type: Interactive, Scenic
- Height: Any
- Opened: 1983
- Location: Fantasyland

Yesterday's Attractions

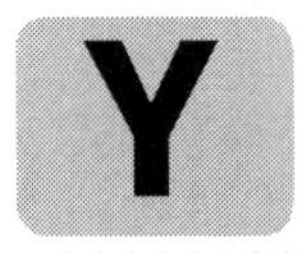

These attractions are no longer around,
but if you look close, pieces of them can still be found.

Yesterday: Fort Wilderness

When looking for attractions of yesterday,
visit Tom Sawyer Island and walk this way.
A fort that kids of all ages could explore,
this fort had things to climb and so much more.

Quick Facts

- Type: Interactive, Scenic
- Height: Any
- Opened: 1956-2003
- Location: Frontierland

Yesterday: Mine Train through Nature's Wonderland

When walking toward Fantasyland on Big Thunder Trail,
look to your left to see what's left of this rail.
This train ride once rode by geysers, cacti, and bears.
Ride its faster replacement—Thunder Mountain—if you dare.

Quick Facts

- Type: Scenic
- Height: Any
- Opened: May 28, 1960, to January 2, 1977 (opened from 1956–1959 as Rainbow Caverns Mine Train)
- Location: Frontierland

Z

Zebras

When you're looking for something that starts with a "Z",
these Jungle Cruise animals are a sight to see.
Their black-and-white stripes make them stand out.
As you pass them in your boat, give them a shout.

Quick Facts

- Type: Scenic
- Location: Adventureland (Jungle Cruise)

Photo Match

In the pages that follow, find photos of magical places.
Guessing their land will put smiles on your faces.
Pay attention to the details as you look at each one.
Flip the book upside down for the answer when you're done!

Outside of the Enchanted Tiki Room, Adventureland

To the left of Harbour Galley, Critter Country

Above the shops, Main Street, U.S.A.

The back streets of New Orleans Square

Near Pluto's Dog House, Mickey's Toontown

Backside of Sleeping Beauty Castle, Fantasyland

Flag pole dedication plaque, Frontierland

Tomorrowland Train Station, Tomorrowland

Trivia Time

Now that you're a Disneyland expert through and through,
it's time to put that knowledge to the test with quizzes just for you!
Take your time to let the answers come out of the blue,
Or you can flip back through the pages for help, too!

Character Match

Disneyland is home to Mickey Mouse and so many more.
Following characters is a great way to explore!
Below, match the character to their Disneyland home town.
When you think you've got them all, turn the page upside down.

Br'er Rabbit	Fantasyland
Buzz Lightyear	Mickey's Toontown
Indian Jones	Main Street, U.S.A.
Tom Sawyer	Tomorrowland
Captain Jack Sparrow	Frontierland
Walt Disney	Adventureland
Mickey Mouse	New Orleans Square
Mr. Toad	Critter Country

Br'er Rabbit—Critter Country, Buzz Lightyear—Tomorrowland, Indiana Jones—Adventureland, Tom Sawyer—Frontierland, Captain Jack Sparrow—New Orleans Square, Walt Disney—Main Street, U.S.A., Mickey Mouse—Mickey's Toontown, Mr. Toad—Fantasyland

Attraction Match

Use the Quick Facts and try your hand
at matching these attractions to their land.
If you're clever and figure them out,
Turn the page upside down and give a shout!

Haunted Mansion
Splash Mountain
Jungle Cruise
The Disney Gallery
Big Thunder Ranch
Gadget's Go Coaster
"it's a small world"
Space Mountain

Main Street, U.S.A.
Adventureland
New Orleans Square
Critter Country
Frontierland
Fantasyland
Tomorrowland
Mickey's Toontown

Haunted Mansion—New Orleans Square, Splash Mountain—Critter Country, Jungle Cruise—Adventureland, The Disney Gallery—Main Street, U.S.A., Big Thunder Ranch—Frontierland, Gadget's Go Coaster—Mickey's Toontown, "it's a small world"—Fantasyland, Space Mountain—Tomorrowland

Walt Disney Quiz

Walt Disney was one amazing man.
Let's see if you can be his ultimate fan.
Use the introduction to give you a clue.
The answers are at the bottom of the page, too.

Q1: What childhood town of Walt Disney was the inspiration for Main Street, U.S.A?

a) Shingle Springs, California b) Marceline, Missouri c) Portland, Oregon

Q2: What year was Walt Disney born?

a) 1955 b) 1901 c) 1922

Q3: What state did Walt Disney move to before creating Snow White?

a) New York b) Nevada c) California

Q4: What year did Walt Disney open Disneyland?

a) 1901 b) 1965 c) 1955

Bonus: How many lands does Disneyland currently have?

a) 8 b) 10 c) 5

A1: b) Marceline, Missouri, A2: b) 1901, A3: c) California, A4: c) 1955, Bonus: a) 8

Glossary

AUDIO-ANIMATRONICS
A non-living figure which can move and make noise.

ATTRACTION
Disney's term for rides and shows.

BOUTIQUE
A small shop.

DARK RIDE
An attraction that takes riders by vehicle into a dark, indoor environment.

DESTINATION
An exciting place to visit.

DIORAMA
A life-size exhibit.

"DIP"
The liquid used in *Who Framed Roger Rabbit* that could melt toons.

FASTPASS
Tickets which can be used to return to rides at a certain time and board almost immediately.

INTERACTIVE
Requires some physical action.

QUEUES
Lines to wait for an attraction or show.

REFURBISHMENT
Fixing or improving an attraction.

SCHWEITZER FALLS
A waterfall named for Dr. Albert Schweitzer, a famous medical missionary.

THRILL RIDE
An exciting ride, usually a roller coaster, that goes fast or down steep hills.

TURRET
A small tower, usually on a castle.

APPENDIX A

Restaurants

Aladdin's Oasis

- Type: Grab and Go
- Serves: Fantasmic! On the Go Picnics
- Location: Adventureland

Bengal Barbecue

- Type: Counter
- Serves: BBQ Skewers
- Location: Adventureland

Big Thunder Ranch Barbecue

- Type: Sit Down
- Serves: BBQ
- Location: Frontierland

Blue Bayou Restaurant

- Type: Sit Down
- Serves: Upscale Cajun
- Location: New Orleans Square

Café Orleans

- Type: Sit Down
- Serves: Cajun/Creole
- Location: New Orleans Square

Carnation Café

- Type: Sit Down
- Serves: American, Breakfast
- Location: Main Street, U.S.A.

Clarabelle's Frozen Yogurt

- Type: Counter
- Serves: Salads, Sandwiches, Ice Cream
- Location: Mickey's Toontown

Club 33

- Type: Sit Down
- Serves: Upscale American
- Location: New Orleans Square

Daisy's Diner

- Type: Counter
- Serves: American, Pizza
- Location: Mickey's Toontown

Edelweiss Snacks

- Type: Counter
- Serves: American (Turkey Legs)
- Location: Fantasyland

French Market Restaurant

- Type: Counter
- Serves: Cajun/Creole
- Location: New Orleans Square

Gibson Girl Ice Cream Parlor

- Type: Counter
- Serves: Ice Cream
- Location: Main Street, U.S.A.

The Golden Horseshoe

- Type: Counter
- Serves: Chicken Strips, Chili
- Location: Frontierland

Harbour Galley

- Type: Counter
- Serves: Baked Potatoes, Salad, Soup
- Location: Critter Country

Hungry Bear Restaurant

- Type: Counter
- Serves: Burgers, Sandwiches
- Location: Critter Country

Jolly Holiday Bakery Café

- Type: Counter
- Serves: Baked Goods, Salads, Sandwiches
- Location: Main Street, U.S.A.

Market House

- Type: Counter
- Serves: Baked Goods, Coffee
- Location: Main Street, U.S.A.

Maurice's Treats

- Type: Counter
- Serves: Pastries
- Location: Fantasyland

Mint Julep Bar

- Type: Counter
- Serves: Beignets, Mint Juleps
- Location: New Orleans Square

Plaza Inn

- Type: Character Meet and Greet, Counter
- Serves: American, Character Dining
- Location: Main Street, U.S.A.

Pluto's Dog House

- Type: Counter
- Serves: Hot Dogs
- Location: Mickey's Toontown

Rancho del Zocalo Restaurante

- Type: Counter
- Serves: Mexican Cuisine
- Location: Frontierland

Redd Rockett's Pizza Port

- Type: Counter
- Serves: Pasta, Pizza, Salad
- Location: Tomorrowland

Refreshment Corner

- Type: Counter
- Serves: American (Hot Dogs, Soup)
- Location: Main Street, U.S.A.

River Belle Terrace

- Type: Counter
- Serves: American, Breakfast Plates
- Location: Frontierland

Royal Street Veranda

- Type: Counter
- Serves: Soup
- Location: New Orleans Square

The Spirit of Refreshment

- Type: Counter
- Serves: Sodas
- Location: Tomorrowland

Stage Door Café

- Type: Counter
- Serves: Corn Dogs, Chicken Nuggets
- Location: Frontierland

Tiki Juice Bar

- Type: Counter
- Serves: Pineapple Flavored Drinks
- Location: Adventureland

Tomorrowland Terrace

- Type: Counter
- Serves: Hamburgers, Sandwiches, Salads
- Location: Tomorrowland

Tropical Imports

- Type: Counter
- Serves: Snacks, Fruit
- Location: Adventureland

Troubadour Tavern

- Type: Counter
- Serves: Bratwurst, Pretzels
- Location: Fantasyland

Village Haus Restaurant

- Type: Counter
- Serves: Pizza, Salad, Sandwiches
- Location: Fantasyland

APPENDIX B

By Land

Adventureland

Attractions

- Enchanted Tiki Room
- Indiana Jones Adventure
- Jungle Cruise
- Tarzan's Treehouse

Restaurants

- Aladdin's Oasis
- Bengal Barbecue
- Tiki Juice Bar
- Tropical Imports

Unique Extras

- Zebras

Critter Country

Attractions

- Davy Crockett's Explorer Canoes
- The Many Adventures of Winnie the Pooh
- Splash Mountain

Restaurants

- Harbour Galley
- Hungry Bear Restaurant

Fantasyland

Attractions

- Alice in Wonderland
- Casey Jr. Circus Train
- Dumbo the Flying Elephant
- Fantasy Faire
- Fantasyland Theatre
- "it's a small world"
- King Arthur Carrousel
- Mad Tea Party
- Matterhorn Bobsleds
- Mr. Toad's Wild Ride
- Peter Pan's Flight
- Pinocchio's Daring Journey
- Pixie Hollow
- Sleeping Beauty Castle (Walkthrough)
- Snow White's Scary Adventures
- Storybook Land Canal Boats

Restaurants

- Edelweiss Snacks
- Maurice's Treats
- Troubadour Tavern
- Village Haus Restaurant

Unique Extras

- Bibbidi Bobbidi Boutique
- Snow White Grotto
- Sword in the Stone

Frontierland

Attractions

- Big Thunder Mountain Railroad
- Big Thunder Ranch
- Frontierland Shootin' Exposition
- The Golden Horseshoe Stage
- Mark Twain Riverboat
- Pirate's Lair on Tom Sawyer Island
- Sailing Ship Columbia

Restaurants

- Big Thunder Ranch Barbecue
- The Golden Horseshoe
- Rancho del Zocalo Restaurante
- River Belle Terrace
- Stage Door Café

Unique Extras

- Fort Wilderness (Yesterday's Attractions)
- Mine Train through Nature's Wonderland (Yesterday's Attractions)
- Petrified Tree

Main Street, U.S.A.

Attractions

- The Disney Gallery
- Disneyland Railroad
- The Disneyland Story Presenting Great Moments with Mr. Lincoln
- Main Street Cinema
- Main Street Vehicles
- Omnibus

Restaurants

- Carnation Café
- Gibson Girl Ice Cream Parlor
- Jolly Holiday Bakery Café
- Market House
- Plaza Inn
- Refreshment Corner

Unique Extras

- City Hall
- Fire Station
- Partners
- Windows

Mickey's Toontown

Attractions

- Chip 'n' Dale Treehouse
- Disneyland Railroad
- Donald's Boat
- Gadget's Go Coaster
- Goofy's Playhouse

- Mickey's House and Meet Mickey
- Minnie's House
- Roger Rabbit's Car Toon Spin

Restaurants

- Clarabelle's Frozen Yogurt
- Daisy's Diner
- Pluto's Dog House

New Orleans Square

Attractions

- Disneyland Railroad
- Haunted Mansion
- Pirates of the Caribbean

Restaurants

- Blue Bayou Restaurant
- Café Orleans
- Club 33
- French Market Restaurant
- Mint Julep Bar
- Royal Street Veranda

Unique Extras

- Club 33

Tomorrowland

Attractions

- Astro Orbitor
- Autopia
- Buzz Lightyear Astro Blasters
- Disneyland Monorail
- Disneyland Railroad
- Finding Nemo Submarine Voyage
- Innoventions
- Magic Eye Theater featuring "Captain EO"
- Space Mountain
- Star Tours—The Adventures Continue
- Starcade

Restaurants

- Redd Rockett's Pizza Port
- The Spirit of Refreshment
- Tomorrowland Terrace

APPENDIX C

By Type

$$

- Bibbidi Bobbidi Boutique
- Frontierland Shootin' Exposition
- Starcade

Character

- Alice in Wonderland
- Buzz Lightyear Astro Blasters
- Chip 'n Dale Treehouse
- Donald's Boat
- Dumbo the Flying Elephant
- Fantasyland Theatre (Mickey and the Magical Map)
- Finding Nemo Submarine Voyage
- Gadget's Go Coaster
- Goofy's Playhouse
- "it's a small world"
- Main Street Cinema
- The Many Adventures of Winnie the Pooh
- Mickey's House and Meet Mickey
- Minnie's House
- Peter Pan's Flight
- Pinocchio's Daring Journey
- Pirates of the Caribbean
- Roger Rabbit's Car Toon Spin
- Sleeping Beauty Castle (Walkthrough)
- Snow White's Scary Adventures

- Star Tours—The Adventures Continue
- Storybook Land Canal Boats
- Tarzan's Treehouse

Character Meet and Greet

- Fantasy Faire (Royal Hall)
- Innoventions
- Mickey's House and Meet Mickey
- Minnie's House
- Pixie Hollow
- Plaza Inn (Character Dining)

Dark Ride

- Alice in Wonderland
- Buzz Lightyear Astro Blasters
- Finding Nemo Submarine Voyage
- Haunted Mansion
- Indiana Jones Adventure
- "it's a small world"
- The Many Adventures of Winnie the Pooh
- Mr. Toad's Wild Ride
- Peter Pan's Flight
- Pinocchio's Daring Journey
- Pirates of the Caribbean
- Roger Rabbit's Car Toon Spin
- Snow White's Scary Adventures
- Space Mountain
- Star Tours—The Adventures Continue

FASTPASS

- Autopia
- Big Thunder Mountain Railroad
- Indiana Jones Adventure
- Roger Rabbit's Car Toon Spin
- Space Mountain
- Splash Mountain
- Star Tours—The Adventures Continue

Interactive

- Astro Orbitor
- Autopia
- Bibbidi Bobbidi Boutique
- Big Thunder Ranch
- Buzz Lightyear Astro Blasters

- Chip 'n' Dale Treehouse
- Davy Crockett's Explorer Canoes
- Donald's Boat
- Dumbo the Flying Elephant
- Fort Wilderness
- Frontierland Shootin' Exposition
- Goofy's Playhouse
- Innoventions
- Mad Tea Party
- Mickey's House and Meet Mickey
- Minnie's House
- Pirate's Lair on Tom Sawyer Island
- Pixie Hollow
- Starcade
- Sword in the Stone
- Tarzan's Treehouse

Land

- Adventureland
- Critter Country
- Fantasyland
- Frontierland
- Main Street, U.S.A.
- Mickey's Toontown
- New Orleans Square
- Tomorrowland

Must be 32" or taller to ride

- Autopia

Must be 35" or taller to ride

- Gadget's Go Coaster

Must be 40" or taller to ride

- Big Thunder Mountain Railroad
- Space Mountain
- Splash Mountain
- Star Tours—The Adventures Continue

Must be 42" or taller to ride

- Matterhorn Bobsleds

Must be 46" or taller to ride

- Indiana Jones Adventure

Original (opened 1955)

Attractions

- Autopia
- Casey Jr. Circus Train
- Disneyland Railroad
- Dumbo the Flying Elephant
- The Golden Horseshoe Stage
- Jungle Cruise
- King Arthur Carrousel
- Mad Tea Party
- Main Street Cinema
- Main Street Vehicles
- Mark Twain Riverboat
- Mr. Toad's Wild Ride
- Peter Pan's Flight
- Sleeping Beauty Castle
- Snow White's Scary Adventures
- Storybook Land Canal Boats

Lands

- Adventureland
- Fantasyland
- Frontierland
- Main Street, U.S.A.
- Tomorrowland

Unique eXtras

- City Hall
- Fire Station

Scary

- Haunted Mansion
- Indiana Jones Adventure
- Matterhorn Bobsleds
- Mr. Toad's Wild Ride
- Pinocchio's Daring Journey
- Pirates of the Caribbean
- Snow White's Scary Adventures
- Space Mountain

Scenic

- City Hall
- The Disney Gallery

- Fire Station
- Fort Wilderness
- Lines
- Mine Train through Nature's Wonderland
- Partners
- Petrified Tree
- Sleeping Beauty Castle
- Snow White Grotto
- Sword in the Stone
- Windows
- Zebras

Show

- The Disneyland Story Presenting Great Moments with Mr. Lincoln
- Enchanted Tiki Room
- Fantasy Faire (Royal Theatre) -Live
- Fantasyland Theatre (Mickey and the Magical Map)—Live
- The Golden Horseshoe Stage –Live
- Magic Eye Theater featuring "Captain EO"
- Main Street Cinema

Spinning

- Astro Orbitor
- Buzz Lightyear Astro Blasters
- Dumbo the Flying Elephant
- King Arthur Carrousel
- Mad Tea Party
- Mr. Toad's Wild Ride
- Roger Rabbit's Car Toon Spin

Thrill Ride (Small Drops)

- Big Thunder Mountain Railroad
- Gadget's Go Coaster
- Indiana Jones Adventure
- Matterhorn Bobsleds
- Pirates of the Caribbean
- Star Tours—The Adventures Continue

Thrill Ride (Large Drops)

- Space Mountain
- Splash Mountain

Transportation

- Disneyland Monorail
- Disneyland Railroad
- Main Street Vehicles
- Omnibus

Water

- Davy Crockett's Explorer Canoes
- Finding Nemo Submarine Voyage
- "it's a small world"
- Jungle Cruise
- Mark Twain Riverboat
- Pirates of the Caribbean
- Sailing Ship Columbia
- Splash Mountain
- Storybook Land Canal Boats

About the Author

Since nearly being born in Disneyland when her pregnant mother did the splits getting off of King Arthur Carrousel in Fantasyland, Kelly Adamson has been fanatic about all things Disney. As a preschool teacher, Kelly wanted to share that passion for Disneyland by writing a book that her four-and five-year-old students could enjoy with their whole family, and *D is for Disneyland* was born.

When she's not spending time at her "happy place", Kelly lives in northern California with her Prince Charming (husband, Ryan), Little Princess (daughter, Cambria), and furry sidekick (cat, Daisy). She is so grateful for the support of her amazing husband and family who have always had "faith, trust, and a little pixie dust" in her dream of becoming a published author someday, and for her parents, for introducing her to a lifetime love of all things Disney.

About the Publisher

Theme Park Press is the largest independent publisher of Disney and Disney-related pop culture books in the world.

Established in November 2012 by Bob McLain, Theme Park Press has released best-selling print and digital books about such topics as Disney films and animation, the Disney theme parks, Disney historical and cultural studies, park touring guides, autobiographies, fiction, and more.

For our complete catalog and a list of forthcoming titles, please visit:

ThemeParkPress.com

or contact the publisher at:

bob@themeparkpress.com

Theme Park Press Newsletter

For a free, occasional email newsletter to keep you posted on new book releases, new author signings, and other events, as well as contests and exclusive excerpts and supplemental content, send email to:

theband@themeparkpress.com

or sign up at

www.ThemeParkPress.com

More Books from Theme Park Press

Theme Park Press publishes dozens of books each year for Disney fans and for general and academic audiences. Here are just a few of our titles. For the complete catalog, including book descriptions and excerpts, please visit:

ThemeParkPress.com

2015
A Tale of
Two
Resorts
COMPARING DISNEYLAND
AND WALT DISNEY WORLD:
A TRAVELER'S
REFERENCE
Kristi Fredericks

THE
RIDE DELEGATE
Memoir of a Walt Disney World VIP Tour Guide
Annie Salisbury

A Historical Tour of
Walt Disney World
Jungle Cruise
Pirates of the Caribbean
Enchanted Tiki Room
Crystal Palace
Main Street, U.S.A.
Carousel of Progress
Tomorrowland
VOLUME I
ANDREW KISTE

Brittany
EARNS
HER
EARS
My Secret Walt Disney World
Cast Member Diary
BRITTANY DICOLOGERO
Earning Your Ears: Volume Five

"Prepare to be enchanted, bewildered and mesmerized by this beat-by-beat account of the Haunted Mansion's creation." Guillermo del Toro, Award-winning film director

The Unauthorized Story of
Walt Disney's
Haunted Mansion

Jeff Baham

Foreword by Rolly Crump

Made in the USA
San Bernardino, CA
19 December 2019

61757871R00075